Rebellious Thinking

"A rebel's thought, a seeker's silence."
..Consciously Humane Rebel as a Warrior Yogi..
: Dhivo

(Dinesh Dilip Talekar)

..Path of understanding via conscious karma towards divine unknown..

Publication : D Innovation Media (Dhivo)

+91 7040038881 | DhivoYoga@gmail.com | Dhivo.in | Dhivo.org

ISBN: 978 – 81 – 932651 – 2 - 3

Price : INR 300

"If you read this book, Rebellious Thinking by Dhivo, before leaving this planet earth, this deeply humane book of experienced insight may transform you into a new kind of human being filled with more Creativity, Compassion,

Consciousness and more over more deeper Understanding about the Higher Values of life..."

--

The Five Greatest Teachings of the Bhagavad Gita — In Dhivo's Eyes

1. Man is both his friend and his foe…
He holds the key to his own liberation.
By walking the path of Karma-Phala Sannyasa Yoga, (Yoga of detaching from the fruits of the action)
Or uniting the roads of wisdom, meditation, devotion and action, (union of Ways of Gyan, Dhyan, Bhakti, Karma)
He can become his own eternal ally —
A companion lit by inner light.

2. Act with the same fire as the ambitious…
But remain untouched by the flames.
Pour your whole being into action —
Yet hold no claim to the fruit.
Be like the silent river:
It flows fiercely,

But never grasps the shores it kisses.

3. Let your action be a flowering of understanding…
Invent not for pride,
But for the upliftment of all life.
Let your thinking serve creation,
Let your doing be a prayer in motion.
This is the Gita's call to the mindful revolutionary
—
The Karma Yogi whose work blesses the world.

4. Sattva, Rajas, Tamas — the three ropes of nature…
Watch them. Know them. But do not be bound.
Walk the inner fire where the gunas dissolve.
Be the witness —
The one who sees clearly,
And chooses freedom over identification.

5. Seek to know thyself, with reverence and rigor…
Not as an ego to be polished,
But as a soul to be uncovered.
And in that knowing,
Let your gaze turn toward the Infinite.
Let meditation not be escape,
But a return —
To the One you've always been. :– Dhivo

Dhivo's Disruptively New Perspective for Today's Youth

By Dhivo (Dinesh Talekar)

Today's youth can no longer remain just KarmaYogis (On the Path of Karma / Action).
Why? Because the definition of a KarmaYogi may be misunderstood —
Reduced, perhaps, to mere doing, without deeper knowing.

A luminous path now calls them forward —
To become Dhyan-Karma Yogi Yuva (Meditator Selfless-Dutiful Actioner Youth)—
Youth anchored not only in action,
But in awareness.

Action will arise naturally —
For energy, enthusiasm, and drive are the very pulse of youth.
But energy without awareness
Is like a blazing fire burning in the wrong direction.

It risks being consumed
By ego, indulgence, and the darkness of ignorance.

This is why
Jośh (passion) must now be held in the arms of Hośh (consciousness).
Karma must be married to the wisdom born of meditation.

Yet the path of "Dhyan" is not easy.
Youth may not easily walk its silent corridors.
They must embrace life's struggles as tapasya —
And take up the full discipline of Ashtanga Yoga.

Through experience and experimentation,
They will come to taste true meditation.
And from that stillness
Shall rise Karma of enduring growth —
Rooted in inner silence, blossoming into outer strength.

To awaken this transformation,
We must rouse the dormant youth consciousness
And begin anew the sacred work of Yuva Shakti Nirman —
The creation of awakened youth. - Dhivo

Understanding Too :

A person of Understandingfulness...

Some people are truly good at heart,
yet sometimes, they act in ignorance.
Likewise, some possess vast knowledge,
but fail to show basic wisdom in life.

To have knowledge is essential.
To have a kind heart is a blessing.
But along with both,
wisdom — grounded, timely, and thoughtful — is just as vital.

When a person considers the situation and timing,
thinks with awareness, and then decides
with a heartful understanding,
such action reflects the true mark of being human.
— Dhivo

Uprooting from Roots:

We keep talking only about trimming the branches and the withered leaves.
No one is even thinking about uprooting the problem from its roots.

Then tell me — how will a monstrous stigma like "rape" ever be erased from humanity? — Dhivo

---

!! I Am Nothing !!
Vantage Note from the Underground

It seems… that whatever you people think about me is probably true.
Indeed, perhaps no one as uneducated as me exists in this world today.
Yes, even I feel I am utterly mad — a complete lunatic.
If ignorance and madness have any limits,
then maybe I am the very embodiment of those limits.
In fact, even these two words might fall short in describing me.

And yes — by calling me "mad" or "uneducated", you might just be insulting those words themselves.
So go ahead, coin a new name for me —
one that suits a being of the grand, grotesque darkness of Kaliyuga.

Back in the day, perhaps it was easier —
People branded Lao Tzu, Mahavira, Kabir, Nanak, and the likes as madmen, illiterates.

They even crucified Jesus and Mansoor,
declaring them insane.

But today…
someone like me, this hyper-madman, might not even find a place among them.
You'd probably need to come up with an entirely new kind of punishment for me.

Yet still, O my Beloved Divine…
In the midst of this madness and ignorance,
I want to say one thing with absolute intensity —
As vast as your treasure of wisdom and love may be,
my longing to receive it is equally vast.

And yet, it seems that even if I were to drink up
the oceans of the entire Milky Way galaxy,
my thirst — this thirst of madness and ignorance — may never be quenched.

That is why…
I truly feel I am nothing.
No matter how much I read,
No matter how much I know,
No matter how wildly I express myself —
I remain… nothing. — Dhivo

You may not understand our language so quickly…
After all, you seem like a traditionalist, don't you?

Some will say: "Reply to a brick with a stone."
Some will say: "Respond to stone with love."
And others might insist: "Iron cuts iron."

But my friend —
If we reply to a brick with a stone, there will be blood on both sides.
And if we try to answer the stone with love —
remember, this is a Kaliyuga stone —
dead, lifeless, unfeeling.
And perhaps… your love too might be of the same Kaliyuga kind.

Does your love hold the strength to melt a stone into wax?
Can you truly love like Meera, Mahavira, or Nanak?

And as for iron cutting iron —
think for a moment:
To cut iron, we must descend to its level, become iron ourselves.
Which means…
neither stone will help,
nor Kaliyugi love, nor even iron.

But yes — if you truly wish to cut iron, become a diamond.
As a diamond,
not just stones — even mountains can be cut.

And if you must love —
then what heart could be greater than that of a diamond,
born out of coal, forged through pressure, pain, and time?
A heart like that can surely reach another stone's soul,
and even understand its pain. — DHIVO

Pointing one finger at others :

They say — when you point one finger at someone, three fingers point back at you…

I don't understand —
why do people keep telling me things I already know?

They say, "You're mad!"
Well, my friend, I know that in your eyes, I am mad.
But did I ever say that your eyes, your thinking, are the real madness?

Take a moment…
look within yourself.

You'll be terrified — maybe even faint —
seeing the monstrous madness growing inside.

If my laughing, loving, playing, joking, and spreading joy
seems like madness to you —
then what do you call your so-called seriousness?
Your pretentious gravity?
Binding people in the chains of a so-called society?

Tell me — isn't that a deeper, darker madness? – DHIVO

If the happiness of others brings us joy,
then know this —
we are truly close to life.
But if their happiness awakens our jealousy or ego,
then understand —
we are still dwelling in darkness. – Dhivo

If you cannot inspire even just two people around you,
then your so-called "leadership"
isn't worth even two pennies in the pages of golden history. — DHIVO

Beauty lies in the eyes of the beholder…
The truly unfortunate one is
the person whose eyes see only ugliness. - Dhivo

The Divine wished to paint your life with vibrant colors…
But you —
you never dared to step out of your nest.

Showers of life's blessings were falling all around…
But you —
you just wouldn't let go of the darkness you cling to. – Dhivo

---

Dwij (Twice Borned) :
Being born was merely the possibility of life…
But the real life —
that, you were meant to earn, to awaken into.

When will you truly understand
the 'Dvija' of India — the twice-born,
and the 'Resurrected' Christ?

You've missed the essence of life many times before…
But if this time too,
you fail to pierce through the darkness,
then yes —

you will be born again and again…
and it may take a thousand lifetimes
just to truly live even one.

Remember this, my fellow traveler in time —
One birth, we receive from our parents…
But the second birth —
that, we must take from within ourselves. – Dhivo

You speak of art and literature from one side of your mouth,
and from the other, you consume flesh without hesitation...

This is no different than —
weaving poems about a mother's love and tenderness on one hand,
while earning your livelihood through prostitution on the other.

Art and literature are meant to be rivers of love and humanity —
but you have turned them into mere mistresses
for your mind's indulgences and ego-pleasures.

A true artist is one whose essence mirrors that of Nanak, Mahavira, and the Buddha —
but you've turned the artist into an ornament of your ego and ignorance.

Yes, perhaps you've created a golden pond through your art,
but do you not realize —
that at the same time, you've been spitting an ocean of savagery and inhumanity?

The gap between your words and your actions
is not just the distance between the earth and sky —
it's the chasm between the underworld and the heavens.

Paradox can be beautiful —
but only when it exists like the relationship between the navel, the mind, and the heart.

There is still time —
Let go of pride and darkness.
Reconnect with the timeless, truthful art and literature
that overflow with love, awareness, and compassion.

The journey of art is one where
God steps out of Himself to become Divine...
Where the soul of God swims through the ocean of literature,
and merges with the Supreme.

Come, let us become true lovers of art,
authentic creators of literature,

and lead the world once again
toward a new, sacred Mahavishva — the Greater World.

With love, — Dhivo

"Misunderstanding"

My friend,
Please don't live in misunderstanding.
I will never lie to you,
nor will I ever hide anything from you.

But believe me when I say —
there's a deep valley ahead.
And yet, you refuse to accept it.

I haven't said anything false.
But if you're standing just two steps behind the truth,
you won't see the abyss from there.
That doesn't make me wrong.

So, I say this:
Let the right time come.
Explore the truth fully.
Then, if you must, blame me.

Where you stand,
and those who've told you things about me —
they all carry half-truths.
People argue for the sake of argument.
Don't get swayed by incomplete stories of others.
Even what your eyes have seen,
and ears have heard —
could be an illusion.

I know that in this delicate situation,
even if I try to help,
you might not accept it.
And that's alright.
But just —
don't carry a misunderstanding.

Wait for the right time.
Try to reach the root of the truth.
And one day will come —
that will light up the golden dawn of our friendship.

Of course the world will burn —
our friendship is so rare, so radiant.
When two beings of God walk together on the path of truth,
that's what we call friendship.

And along this path of truth,
thorns will certainly appear —
conflict, disagreements, tension —

but isn't that the very test of truth?
The fire-test of friendship?

When I look into your heart,
I see a reflection of myself.
You are the mirror in which I see my own soul.
And in the same way,
I too am a mirror for you.
So how can I be angry at myself?
And how could you lie to yourself, or hide from yourself?

My dear friend,
just wipe the dust off the mirror —
and you will witness the truth clearly.
Your misunderstanding will scatter like dust in the wind.

What I see, I will keep warning you about.
It may appear, on the surface,
as though I have a selfish motive —
but know this —
I've stayed back only for you.

Many have told me:
"Why wait? Move on, leap over the valley.
Those who are meant to fall, will fall.
Your shouting won't change a thing."

But I didn't listen to them.
I've stayed —

only for your love.

I wish that those who try to mislead you
could understand my heart…
perhaps then they too would escape the darkness.
But that seems nearly impossible.
They've chained themselves so tightly to their own selfishness —
like a fox entangled in its own cunning.
My dear companion,
Even if your heart resists today,
just remember my words — one day, you will believe them. Always yours — your true friend. - Dhivo

---

"How Tragic It Truly Is…"

How tragically unfortunate it is…
You didn't even realize it —
and yet, you kept living under the burden of school offices and exam files.

You didn't even notice —
you were dragging the weight of 10th, 12th, and graduation,
as if life was nothing but a syllabus to be carried.

You never saw it coming —
when the responsibility of a job began to weigh down your shoulders.
You didn't realize —

when the sorrowful joy of marriage came crashing
onto your chest.

You didn't even notice —
when the weight of raising children began to crush
your spine.
You didn't really live… forgive me —
you were merely being dragged,
suffocating beneath burdens,
cutting through a half-dead life.

And you never knew —
this was a 'Chakravyuh' (the fatal maze of illusion),
and you were neither Abhimanyu nor Arjuna. You didn't know — you were spinning endlessly in circles within a trap that had no real exit.

And beneath the load of ignorance,
your soul cried bloody tears,
while you — forgive me again —
lived and died like an animal,
wandering in darkness... – Dhivo

Life!
Life is right here…
It's in the now, in this very moment…
But we keep searching for it
in the yesterday that has passed,
and the tomorrow yet to come…

And while chasing life
in hopes of finding it,
it silently slips away—
right before our very eyes… – Dhivo

What is Unconsciousness?

(With a gentle smile)
You've spun such a vast illusion of unconsciousness…
Well, let me share at least one form of it with you…

You choose misunderstanding over understanding...
You're quick to hold on to negativity
when it comes to any person, subject, or event...
Without knowing the full truth,
you allow prejudices and false assumptions
to settle in your mind.

Understanding is awareness;
and ignorance has always been unconsciousness.

These unconscious habits
have now seeped into your very bloodstream—
but before it's too late,
before they pierce into the core of your soul…
You must awaken.
You must break the spell of unconsciousness.

To move from darkness toward light,
you must embrace true understanding.

(Again, smiling softly)
The absence of understanding—
that itself is unconsciousness. – DHIVO

A Priceless Question :

How astonishing it is…
that people have no idea,
what to do with this life?.. – Dhivo

"The body, the nature within, and the wisdom to think with heart are the true treasures as a human being..
But even today, man remains confined,
In the wealth of papers & precious metals, and in the estate of bricks & lifeless stones.." – Dhivo

---

"Everyone can sees upto their capacity of physical eyes..
But only a rare few awaken their subtle and far-reaching vision —
The ones we call the philosophers,

The visionaries of time." – Dhivo
--

"The eyes, in all their physical might,
Can only see what lies within their sight.
But rare are those who awaken the subtle and the far —
The seers of truth, the visionaries,
The philosophers who gaze beyond the stars." – Dhivo

"Caution!
Here, those who've grown old in their minds
Are busy turning the youth and children
Into copies of their own —
Serious, rigid, and prematurely aged by tradition." – Dhivo

Joy it is, indeed —
That we celebrate the festival of lamps.
But there's a sorrow that lingers quietly...
Over five thousand years have passed,
And still, only one Ram has walked this land.
While countless lives have been spent
In rituals, offerings, and empty traditions.

Wishing you a truly Enlightened Diwali!
Let the light spread outside — yes —

But only when the lamp of wisdom is lit within." – Dhivo

Advait — Non-Duality

Very few will truly understand me,
But the rare ones who do —
They will never be able to leave me, even if they try.

Not even the red of paan and catechu is this deep,
Nor the blood in anyone's veins this thick,
No butterfly adorned with such colors,
No garden blooming with such wild beauty,
And no setting sun has ever burned so richly —

As the rainbow woven from the hues of my love.

Once you awaken and truly see me —
You won't be able to leave me,
Because you'll no longer remain.
You'll drown in my depths,
Just like a drop dissolving into the ocean.

But this time,
Watch the miracle —
The ocean will dissolve into the drop.

When a consciousness beyond the intellect and heart touches me,

That... will be Advait.
When you step beyond outer youth
And feel the soul's awareness in the heart —
That... will be Advait.
When you melt into the endless horizon
Where sky and earth appear to meet —
That... will be Advait.
When you ride the waves,
Only to sink and be reborn through them —
That... will be Advait.

If you truly know me,
I will take you on a journey into the great unknown.
If you deeply feel me,
I will unveil life's golden secrets for you.
If you grasp the vastness of my being,
I will fold myself into a seed —
The seed fallen from a mighty tree.

Come, become one with me.
I will give you death —
Only to gift you a life never known before.

For I am Death.
And I am Birth.
Throw yourself into the abyss of this death —
And you will be born anew.
A miraculous moment will occur —
The awakening of the Twice-Born.

Two may appear together,
But they are not two.
They are not even one.
They are form and formlessness, many and same.
That is Advait.

Let it be known: Advait is not a concept to be caged.
It is a riddle, a sacred mystery.
Can love ever be trapped in words?
Can the fragrance of a flower be strung into alphabets?
It can only be felt.

So come —
Feel it. Live it.
As if there is no birth, no death,
Only the Infinite, the Boundless — Advait. : Dhivo

Understanding:

Many times, people fail to understand us.
But that's alright — they are, after all, just people.
For it is the individual who understands.
Crowds have no thinking of their own —
Only a person can truly pause and decide with thought.

People believe
That birds belong only in the sky,

And fish must swim only in the sea.

But they fail to see —
What harm is there if a bird dives deep?
And what's wrong if a fish dares to fly?

No — they want everything bound in circles,
No different thoughts,
No new ideas.

We are the kind of humans
Who wish to live for others,
And yet even in that — they see selfishness.

If only they could rise a little above,
They might see a whole other life —
Golden, green, and radiant
Like a rainbow after rain.

But there's still time.
If they wish, they can extend a hand of understanding,
They can spark a change in thought.

And if not —
We will continue to understand them anyway,
As the ocean understands each wave —
Like its own child. — Dhivo

The Absence of Goodness:

The absence of goodness —
Is not evil in itself.
It is merely the lack of light,
Or perhaps...
The quiet presence of a possibility —
That goodness is yet to be born. : — Dhivo

Rebirth Through Struggle:
Your new birth will not come
By escaping struggle and challenges —
But only by diving deep into them,
Fearlessly, fully,
And finding yourself anew within. :— Dhivo

Who is a true youth?

The one who keeps learning, endlessly.
The one who dares to walk into the unknown.
The one with the courage to stand alone.
The one gifted with the brilliance of highest discernment.
The one who strives —
To be rooted in awareness,
Through the stillness of deep meditation. :— Dhivo

The Ecstasy of Life:

When one begins to witness the nature of consciousness itself,
Waves of ecstasy ripple through life,
Spreading fragrance in every direction.

When those waves of joy
Turn into the heart's call toward the unknown,
A monsoon of grace arrives,
And the season of inner rain begins.

When that heartfelt call
Travels beyond the soul — carrying love,
A sacred union with the true beloved takes place.

And when love transcends the soul,
And the lover merges in stillness beyond form,
A timeless Advait is born in life.

True love is a gift from the Divine.
And if that love happens with the Divine —
Such a rare and wondrous union
Can never be fully spoken in words.

When the eyes fill with tears,
And the heart overflows —
When breath to heartbeat, body to soul,
All of it begins to feel Him within...

Then, and only then —
Life begins to truly live itself.
Then, the aliveness of living
Can awaken life once more. - Dhivo

Rare is the True Lover : Dhivo

Very few lovers exist
Who, in love, wish only for the well-being of the other.
For love today —
Has sadly become
A so-called marketplace
Of give and take,
A silent bargain in the name of emotion.

But true love...
It neither demands nor expects —
It simply wishes well.

The Ageing of Thought:

Physical old age begins sometime after fifty...
But in India —
Our thinking begins to grow old
Right from childhood. : Dhivo

Helping the Weak, Not the Will-less

We help the weak learn to stand on their own feet —
But don't come to us as weakness itself,
For then, we may not be able
To help you at all. - : Dhivo

"Keys to Advait Living" or "Treasures of a Complete Life."

A Revelation: Keys to a Life of Advait

Dear friends,
Today, I wish to unveil a secret...

If a few sacred keys come into your hands,
You may unlock that rarest treasure —
A life we might truly call complete,
A life of greatness, beauty, and Advait.

And among those quiet secrets, here are a few:

One — Mastery over your own thoughts, speech, and way of living.
Two — The companionship of wise friends
whose lives are rooted in higher values.
Three —
For a man: the presence of a woman

who is an embodiment of love, deep thought, art, and grace.
For a woman: the presence of a man
who carries love, luminous intellect, bold spirit, and noble action.
Four — A journey into the most wondrous,
unseen corners of the world —
a life of soulful discovery.
These are not mere checklists,
but living mysteries that quietly open the door
to a fulfilled and radiant existence. —Dhivo

The Signs of Greatness:

The making of a truly great being
Is a natural process —
Yes, it will take time…
But the signs of that greatness
Will begin to reveal themselves
Long before the greatness is complete. — Dhivo

Exploring True Education and Human Values:
The Truly Educated, the Truly Human :

One who understands the highest values of life —
Is truly educated.
But one who lives those values
Through their thoughts, words, and actions — Is truly human. — Dhivo

---

A very simple truth…
If you genuinely wish to bring the highest transformation in your life,
then begin by cultivating a balanced positive mindset,
and develop a heart filled with gratitude towards all beings. : Dhivo

---

Yes, It's a simple truth...

If you truly seek a profound shift in your life,
then begin — not with action, but with your inner atmosphere.
Cultivate a balanced, positive way of thinking,
and let your heart be steeped in gratitude for all beings.

For it's not outer achievements but inner alignment that quietly turns the tide of destiny.

When thoughts are steady like a calm flame,
and gratitude flows like a silent river through your being,

life begins to blossom — not just in form, but in essence.

This is the real revolution.
It begins not outside, but within you. : Dhivo

The Guru ...

Your yearning and quest must be deep enough…
Only then will the human life grant you
that sublime, sacred experience.

The Guru...
does not give it to you — He merely becomes the mirror in which your inner fire is revealed. : Dhivo

---

Failures are not rejections… they are revelations.
They whisper —
You need to become even more mature,
and work even harder...

They also gently reveal that
your path is different.

Perhaps the present generation may not understand
the fire of your visionary actions,
nor the brilliance of your future-illuminating thoughts.

And so,
you were never meant to flow with the current —
you were meant to carve your own.

Even if alone,
you must shape your path
and awaken a new dawn through the very force of your being.

You are not a follower of trends.
You are the origin of a new era. : DHIVO

When you do something for others,
its value multiplies infinitely…

But if you do it only for yourself,
you won't even be able
to draw a single drop
from the vast ocean of life.

True worth is born
when your actions flow beyond the self
and touch the shores of someone else's need. : Dhivo

-

A drop drawn for the world is worth more than an ocean hoarded for the self."-Dhivo

---

Curiosity may give us some information,
and even inquiry might offer a glimpse of knowledge —
but until the deep longing of Mumuksha (intense spiritual seeking) awakens within,
we shall neither realize the highest truths of life,
nor begin the true search for our supreme existence. : Dhivo

Kutuhal – Jigyasa – Mumuksha :

Curiosity may give us some information,
and even inquiry might offer a glimpse of knowledge —
but until the deep longing of Mumuksha (intense spiritual seeking) awakens within,
we shall neither realize the highest truths of life,
nor begin the true search for our supreme existence. : Dhivo

In the Game of Life…

Life is like a vast and intricate game —
and within this grand play, we must participate in many smaller games.
But before entering any game, we must consciously set a few things straight:

One, know why and when to begin.
Two, understand the rules — thoroughly.
Three, know the stakes — what you may win, and more importantly, what you may lose.
Four, be aware of when to exit.
Five, choose your games wisely — with selfless clarity and inner balance.
Six, seek such a game in which, whether you win or lose, you still grow and evolve.
Seven, and most of all — never forget,
it's just a game,
a divine drama where you are but a conscious actor on the stage of existence.

Play it sincerely —
but don't mistake the play for the Self, as it is just a stage of drama and you are here as an actor, performer : DHIVO - Yuvashakti Nirman Kendra, Dhivo Yoga Meditation & Spirituality Center

---

According to science, it appears as a shift in hormones.
According to spirituality, it is seen as a play of the three gunas —
Sattva, Rajas, and Tamas.

We merely feel,
"This is what I am thinking right now..."
But that thought
might just be a reflection
of shifting hormonal tides,
or the rising and falling waves of these subtle cosmic qualities.

What seems like our own thinking
may simply be a momentary echo
of nature's invisible dance within us. : DHIVO

A profoundly poetic and deeply introspective piece — blending spiritual awakening, self-realization, and the paradox of knowing and unknowing. It evokes the timeless feeling of "losing oneself to truly find oneself.

When the Buddha Returned Home… — Dhivo

I don't know exactly when this began,
but ever since I became "conscious,"

I've been lost in unconsciousness.

When the world believed I had "come to my senses,"
I was merely asleep —
just like them.

But then, that one moment arrived…
and something within shifted.
For the first time in life,
I truly became aware —
and in that very instant,
I lost all sense of who I was.

Today, I am alive — truly alive.
Before, I had only taken birth.
But now… life has begun,
only after I've dissolved the old self.

When Buddha returned home after twelve long years,
his father said,
"There's still time — you can come back."
But the Buddha replied,
"Look closely, Father…
I am not the one who left this house.
If I were still your son,
perhaps I could return —
but now, I have become someone else.
Returning… is no longer possible."
When Newton caught a glimpse of awareness,

someone praised him:
"You are so wise, so brilliant!"
But Newton humbly responded,
"My friend, whatever I have known
has only taught me one thing —
how little I actually know.
What I've discovered is a drop;
an ocean of knowledge remains untouched.
I remain a humble seeker,
still deeply… unconscious."

Some will lose themselves in knowledge,
some in love.
Some will vanish into the Self,
others into the galaxies & universe.

I don't know where I have disappeared…
But ever since I truly became conscious —
I've been lost. : Dhivo

When everything was going well,
I was merely living… comfortably.

But it was only when pain and struggle surrounded me,
that I created the most meaningful work of my life.

Forgive me…
for it is through sorrow and silence

that I have truly entered into the Karma of Meditation & Creativity. : Dhivo

---

Those who have never walked through the fire of
humanity's trials
are often the ones
who cling to rigid beliefs,
disguising them as religion, caste, or faith.

And worse —
they become messengers not of truth,
but of disturbance,
spreading noise in the name of the sacred. : Dhivo

This quote distills profound yogic wisdom into a fivefold path — a subtle spiritual algorithm that can transform one's inner identity from fragmented ego to Karmayogi...:

Through the fivefold path of
non-doership,
detachment,
understanding,
acceptance,
and creative discovery —

a human being can become their own friend.

And in that rare flowering,
the extraordinary transformation into a Karmayogi
can truly begin. : Dhivo

This thought is a profound reminder that karma is not just economic, but ethical and spiritual. Tried to points out the invisible accounting of daily life — beyond income and expenditure, toward virtue and vice, conscience and consequence.

\---

Whenever we act in life —
be it through daily labor or livelihood —
we are not earning just money.

Along with wealth,
we're also silently accumulating
either merit (punya)
or misdeed (paap) —
sometimes both.
So before you sleep each night,
take a moment.
Reflect on not just what you earned in currency,
but what you deposited
in the unseen ledger
of your conscience.

Let Destiny not feel ashamed

while balancing your account.
Make it easy for her to calculate —
not heavy with regret.: Dhivo

---

a deeply empowering insight — recognizing the limits of fate (prarabdha) while reclaiming the freedom of conscious response.

We may not be able to change our prarabdha (Destiny)—
the karmic script already in motion...
But what we can transform,
is how we respond to life.

Let us rise above mere reactions.
Let us choose a response —
rooted in awareness,
not in habit.

This is how destiny becomes a dialogue,
and we begin to co-create
rather than just endure. : Dhivo

A sharp revealing of the subtle shift from selfless help to selfish expectation — a transformation that exposes the true intent (niyat) behind human behavior.

Intent (Niyat)

Some people begin by appearing selfless —
offering help without asking for anything in return.

But the moment your work starts to bloom,
when success begins to shine through you…
their intentions begin to shift.

Soon, expectations creep in —
not just simple ones,
but grand constructions of self-interest
begin to rise around you.
And what once felt like support
now feels like subtle control. : Dhivo

Radiates the humility of true mastery *— a heartfelt tribute from a teacher, friend, or guide who recognizes the brilliance already present in the other.*

--

I wasn't the one who turned you into gold —
those qualities were already shining within you.

If anything,
it is because of you
that I could become the touchstone.

You didn't need me to become precious —

but I needed you
to become meaningful. : Dhivo

A profound invitation to shift our entire relationship with life *— from consumption to consecration, from craving to gratitude, from indulgence to liberation.*

--

Life is the sacred offering we've received from the Divine.

But how shall we receive this prasād (blessed food)?

With desire?
Or with gratitude?

Shall we treat life as a playground of pleasures
to be merely consumed and exhausted?

Or shall we embrace it
with reverence and responsibility —
as a sacred opportunity
for liberation through grateful action? : Dhivo

Gracefully reveals a harsh truth about human *psychology and social perception — that truth is often judged not by its depth, but by the perceived weight of the speaker.*

--

If someone isn't taken seriously by the world,
then even if they speak a profound truth,
it will still be dismissed lightly.

So often,
it is not what is said that matters most —
but who says it.

Truth, sadly,
is not always heard on the merit of its clarity,
but on the authority of the voice that carries it. : Dhivo

A gentle, yet profound reminder of life's hidden alchemy — where sorrow becomes the soil and struggle the roots, from which the sweet fruit of joy eventually blossoms...

Whenever you taste the fruit of happiness,
do remember to thank your sorrow.

For perhaps,
it was the bitter days,
the harsh experiences,
and the silent struggles —

that became the very roots
from which your blossoms of bliss

have grown. : Dhivo

***Reflects a deep yogic insight** — that relativity and proportion are not just scientific principles, but inner instruments through which we can weave a balanced, wise life.*

--

Through relativity and proportion,
we can bring balance to life —
and with mindful worthiness,
we can skilfully weave
the intricate threads of joy and sorrow
into a harmonious tapestry.

For it is not about escaping life's contrasts,
but learning to measure, hold, and merge them
with awareness. : Dhivo

Wherever We Are — Is Where Awakening Awaits

Wherever we stand —
in time, in space, in spirit —
whatever surrounds us, even all of it,
may well be a hidden hand
guiding us toward
our own humane liberation.

But for that grace to be felt,
we must awaken three sacred senses:

Relativity — the art of perspective,
Harmony — the balance of being,
Dialogue — the soulful bridge
between what is and what could be.

Only then do ordinary moments
turn into portals of redemption. – Dhivo

The Subtle Science of Inner Harmony

"Wherever we stand — in time, in space, in spirit — whatever surrounds us, even all of it, may well be a hidden hand guiding us toward our own humane liberation. But for that grace to be felt, we must awaken three sacred senses: relativity, harmony, and dialogue." — Dhivo

---

Time, the Invisible Guru

"To walk with time does not merely mean to follow trends or deadlines.
It means to extract meaning — churned through the alchemy of balance, relativity, and goodwill."
— Dhivo

What Does It Mean to Flow with Time?

To walk with time
is not merely to adjust your pace.
It is to churn its meaning —
like the ocean was churned
to reveal nectar hidden beneath chaos.

To truly flow with time
is to extract its essence
through the alchemy of balance,
the lens of relativity,
and the spirit of goodwill.

Balance keeps us cantered when life sways.
Relativity gives us vision beyond black and white.
Goodwill allows us to meet change,
not as a threat, but as a companion.

This is the inner art —
not of chasing the clock,
but of harmonizing with the rhythm
of Time as a Teacher. : Dhivo

The Wings of Inner Ascent

Through the wandering of spiritual rituals
and the pursuit of pilgrimages and prayers,
we keep searching merely for comfort and joy…

But if we open the wings of goodwill and wise discernment,
then — in truth —
pain, yearning, and sorrow
become the very alchemical forces
that give airplane-like speed
to our inner journey. — Dhivo

They may or may not possess spiritual powers…
But tell me —
Is your soul's exam
meant to be copied and solved by someone else,
instead of you living and answering it yourself? — Dhivo

The moment we realize:

that this entire play
is woven through vibrations, waves, and feelings,
we begin to embody
the true energies of
gratitude, forgiveness, surrender, and detachment into our lives — naturally, silently, deeply. — Dhivo

---

The question is not of bodily health…
nor of mental pleasure…
nor even of religious beliefs.

The real question is —
Does your soul truly desire
to snatch away the body —
naturally gifted to another soul —
and find pleasure in its suffering,
simply for the taste of meat? — Dhivo

"**Whether non-vegetarianism is right or wrong** — that may still be debated…

But when one tortures and kills another sentient being —
or gets it killed —
just to satisfy bodily pleasure or sensory indulgence...

What debate remains in that?" — Dhivo
--

The debate over whether eating meat is right or wrong may continue…
But the act of killing or causing to kill a sentient being,
simply for bodily indulgence —
What kind of debate is needed for that? — Dhivo

"**You may believe you are just eating flesh…**

But what's truly being consumed — is your own destiny." — Dhivo

--

From a spiritual perspective…
all beings you wish to consume
for your sensory pleasure
— are already dead —
long before you touch them.

Their deaths are written
into the cyclical time-pattern of existence.

But if any harm shall now truly occur…
If any death must now be accounted for…
It is not theirs.
It will be your karma… your destiny… that dies.
— Dhivo

The question is not about your religious beliefs
—
especially if you've kept them locked away for centuries…

And even then — it won't be a real question
if your inner soul has chosen
to stay trapped in its own self-woven web.

And still — no question will arise
if you keep pretending to be asleep…

Or if you’ve already decided
to strike the axe on your own feet.

Or even worse —
if you've chosen to become
your own greatest enemy…

Then neither the question…
nor the act of questioning…
shall hold any meaning. — Dhivo

Not just religious…
but any belief —
it’s perfectly fine to accept it
after testing it against human values.

Just remember one thing —

You have only believed it…
not yet known it. — Dhivo
--
"It’s okay to believe — just don’t forget that it’s not yet your knowing.— Dhivo

---

If you eat meat,
ask yourself three unfinished questions:

1. Do I truly need to eat it?

2. Have I been born as a human without human sensitivity?

3. Am I under the influence of tamasic (dark, inert) tendencies?

If your answers waver…
perhaps it's not your body —
but your soul that's hungry for awakening. — Dhivo

"My ancestors ate meat…" "I've eaten it since childhood…"

Such arguments fall apart — the moment you remember:

You have your own mind. You have a living heart.

And not just your body, even your thoughts are evolving.

Let them. Let your thinking grow beyond your habits. — Dhivo

At least once a year — do a gentle diagnosis…
not of your body, but of your habits.

Observe your patterns — before they turn into knots of destiny.

What you repeat unconsciously can one day repeat itself karmically.

Heal it… while it's still a habit. Not after it becomes your fate. — Dhivo

---

Sometimes…
looking back becomes necessary —
not out of regret,
but out of clarity.

Especially when what looks like “light” ahead,
hides a subtle darkness…

And behind you —
karmic knots still pulling,
regrets still echoing.

Looking back isn’t weakness.
It’s realignment.

Because the past, when faced consciously,
can clear the fog of the future. — Dhivo

Beware! There have always been so-called "custodians" —
who bend facts to fit their beliefs,
create confusion and noise through clever debates,
and use the name of faith or tradition
to mislead the masses.

But the day will come —
when humans are compared
with more evolved extraterrestrial beings…

And then — these inhuman ideologies
and their loudest advocates
will shrink into such irrelevance,
that they may not even dare
to show their face in the light of truth. — Dhivo

The Truly Educated, the Truly Human

One who understands the highest values of life —
Is truly educated.
But one who lives those values
Through their thoughts, words, and actions —
Is truly human. — Dhivo (Dinesh Talekar)

One part of the mind says —
Go ask them,
Share with them — the rights and wrongs
of their own joys and sorrows...
But the other part of the mind whispers —
What if they misunderstand?
What if the words reach their ego instead... — Dhivo

If That is not within you and me,
Then it's not even there —

Not in the place, nor the direction,
Nor the deity where you bow your head…

But if we carry even a drop of pure devotion within,
Then That will also be found —
Even in the place where nothing else exists... — Dhivo

In truth, many of those you consider "bad"
are merely directionless souls, who aren't truly bad — not even in difficult circumstances…
Even a lion, a dog, or an ant may attack
if provoked — just like what often happens
these days on social media... — Dhivo

We cannot even breathe or sleep entirely by our own will…
We may be able to swallow food,
but we don't truly possess the power to digest it...

And yet — we clothe that unimaginable Force
in the rigid robes of names, cultures, and creeds,
claiming ownership over it
as if we've understood everything
and there's nothing left to discover... — Dhivo

If someone crossed our path just once or twice in life,
and we never met them again —
still, they must exist somewhere, in some corner of this vast existence...

Taking that same principle to a deeper truth —
Those who leave their bodies behind,
must also be somewhere,
somehow, still present...

And perhaps, on the strength of this quiet hope,
we shall keep moving forward
in the journey of evolution,
meeting and parting — again and again... — Dhivo

Book by Dhivo — Rebellious Thinking
Thoughts with such depth —
they might touch your heart,
or settle into your mind,
or at times, even
fly right over your head...

But at the very least — just once,
they'll surely make you pause and think. : Dhivo

“The path that promises gain,
or the journey that assures rewards —
almost everyone would choose that...

But the path where loss seems more likely than gain,
where even getting something is uncertain —

only a rare few dare to walk that way...” — Dhivo

If we truly wish to rise in life,
or take the reins of our life into our own hands,
then we must certainly become filled with awareness...

Otherwise, even in a state of unconsciousness,
insects and animals too are somehow just existing,
aren't they? — Dhivo

What do you really see?

Isn’t it astonishing…
that even with two eyes,
we often live in blindness?
And even when we do see something,
each of us sees it differently...

One sees a Muslim dying,

another sees a Jew dying...
Some see a Ukrainian fall,
others a Russian in pain...

But what no one seems to hear —
is the voice that quietly says:
"Look… a human being like us is dying."

We see people taking sides —
with this side or that,
but why don't we see the ones
standing with innocent lives,
regardless of their side?

On one hand, we reach new heights in space,
and on the other, we plunge into the depths of cruelty.
Where does this hypocrisy come from, in mankind?

Even with two wide eyes,
why can't we see —
a dying, innocent human... 😟🙏 — Dhivo

If, in the material world,

we use a microscope to observe the tiniest elements,

and a telescope to see the farthest distances —

Then in the inner world,

to reach the Supreme Subtle Essence (Para-Tattva),

shouldn't we too use the instruments of

Knowledge and Meditation? — Dhivo

Yes, as if
life itself is a battlefield...
But some leap into it
in unconsciousness,
while others enter it
with awareness.

First, the unaware rush in blindly,
and then — out of necessity,
the aware are forced to dive in
just to save them… — Dhivo

No, there won't be any benefit for you.
If you give up meat, it might even feel like a loss —

Your tongue will crave,

Your body might not seem as strong,
at least not by your usual standards...

But —
maybe, just maybe,
a life will be spared —
an animal, a bird,
won't have to suffer and die.

Perhaps you're right —
If someone's life is saved,
if no being has to die in agony,
then you personally might gain nothing at all...
— Dhivo #JaisaAnnVaisaMann

Even if we fail to become a perfect Karmayogi,
but if we keep making a sincere effort to act with aware engagement in action,
and maintain a natural detachment from the results,
then at the very least —
we shall truly remain Human. — Dhivo

What should the upbringing of a youth be like?

First — to become useful (UpaYogi),
Then — to grow into being supportive (Co-Yogi),
And eventually — to strive towards becoming a Yogi... — Dhivo

Who says it doesn't matter
how far you've travelled outwardly?
Maybe that's true...

But whether you've begun the
inner journey or not —
that not only matters,
it actually defines your very existence. — Dhivo

If you're a human, then first — seek the humanity within yourself.
Only when true humanness awakens from within, should you begin to move forward… toward the Divine. — Dhivo

---

"Misunderstanding" spreads so easily — from one mind to another, like an infection... But when it comes to sharing understanding, it takes every ounce of effort, every bit of strength — to truly make it reach. — Dhivo

---

Don't act with the thought — "What will I get?"
Instead, act with the spirit — "What can I give?"

Then the very feeling of gratitude will strive to turn you into a sun —
radiating light, warmth, and life. — Dhivo

With death in front of you... If we live not by weighing gain or loss, honor or insult,
but by keeping our own death in clear sight —
then we will truly live, fully and fearlessly… And perhaps, we won't even get entangled in the bondage of karma.
— Dhivo

Protect the delicate union of relationships —
For a nest takes great effort to build…

But remember —
we are neither the birds who build it,
nor the nest itself.
At most, we may be just a single straw
used in its making…

So how can we ever
think of ourselves as more than that?
— Dhivo

"Friendship" — by Dhivo

Those who doubt whether their name lives in someone's heart,
are usually the ones who pursue diplomatic, time-pass friendships,
forever searching for their name in papers, posters, or videos…

But those who trust in the purity of their own heart —
who know their friendship is genuine and selfless —
they don't need their name to appear anywhere.
It doesn't matter to them.

And truthfully, a heart-born friendship can't exist with just anyone.
This marketplace, full of so-called 'friends',
reveals its true colours when the crowd begins to disperse…

Friendships with self-interest are always just that —
friendships of interest.
While friendships with no interest at all —
are the ones that are truly called friendship.

In both, the friendship often disappears…
but the interest — it never does.

So what kind of friendship is real?
What is friendship, then?

Some chapters of life cannot be defined —
and friendship is one of them.
Friendship is a purest emotion,
a noble sentiment —
a natural union of discerning intellect
and compassionate sensitivity.

True friendship is beyond all divisions.
If friendship exists, humaneness exists in humanity.
If not, then perhaps we are just a human species,
not humans in the true sense.

Those who know, know —
that the Supreme Reality may not hunger for rituals,
but it hungers for "Bhava" — the essence, the emotion.
And that "Bhava" is seen in the friendship of Krishna-Arjuna,
of Krishna-Sudama.

Let the spirit of friendship express itself —
Because that state where two friends dissolve
in pure Maitri Bhava (spiritual companionship) —
that is called Friendship.

But if friendship is just about time-pass
or eating and drinking together —
then what meaning does trust hold?
What does standing by someone in tough times mean?
What does it mean to call or message first,
just to check in, without any reason?

There are people who won't even ask for a glass of water
when you meet —
But those who understand the worth of friendship
know that true friendship has no price.

Yes, friendship is sometimes tested unknowingly —
through misunderstandings or unfortunate timing.
Sometimes, it may even be affected by envy...

But true friendship —
needs no watchful eye,
and can never truly be ignored.

And how can you not trust a true friend?
Because the other name of trust itself is friend.

When that friend becomes trust itself,
you no longer need to try to trust them —
You simply do. — Dhivo

Here We Are — So Let's Live Fully, Right Here... — Dhivo

Since we're here,
let's savor this place,
dive deep into life itself,
and live it wholeheartedly, with life — in life.

Even if we hustle, chase, or crawl to reach "there" someday,
what if, upon arrival,
we find death waiting, instead of life?
Can we ever be sure what lies ahead?

So come, dear friends...
Let others say what they will —
we'll keep walking alongside life,
sip by sip,
sharing this rare nectar of existence
with open hearts.

But truly,
who else is even here?
If we look closely,
in every atom, there's only silence —
If we believe, there's an "other"...
If we know, there's only non-duality.

It's just a matter of attention —

until attention becomes awareness —
and we realize:
perhaps the place we long to reach...
we've already arrived, unknowingly.

So come —
let's slow down, right now.
Pause, meet, and truly live.
Yes — here, now, in this very moment,
let's drink this moment down...

Who knows what tomorrow holds?
So maybe not tomorrow, but this moment,
this moment... or just a few moments —
let's live them fully.
Let's taste the joy of being alive.

— Dhivo - Together we can — make life more Humane, Healthy, Happy & Harmonious.

Attached Yet Detached — Dhivo

""People will always talk — it's simply what they do."
..."
So let them talk.

Why waste this diamond-like life
worrying about what others will say?

Living for others,
and living because of what others might think —
these are worlds apart.

The first birth is given by our parents.
The second, we must give ourselves.
In Indian spirituality, that's called a Dvija — the twice-born one.

But truth is —
most people just do what feels right to them in the moment.
And that's okay too.

Some learn through others' experiences,
while some won't learn until they fall into the pit themselves.
No matter what —
the law of cause and effect never fails.
What you sow, you shall reap —
if not today, then someday.

So, is any path really wrong?
Not really —
some are just different.

Whenever you awaken,
that's your sunrise.

“Asato Ma Sadgamaya”
(Lead me from untruth to truth...) — Dhivo

Who is really living this life?..
To say "we are living life" might actually be a contradiction...
Just take a closer look at yourself —

Who is truly living in your name?
Isn’t it your prejudices, your habits, and all those unconscious beliefs
that are carrying out the business of living on your behalf? — Dhivo

---

The value of time and the timely ones —
One who understands the value of time in time,
is not filled with regret or remorse on their deathbed,
but rather with gratitude and thankfulness... — Dhivo

The declaration of the Chhāndogya Upanishad — “Tat Tvam Asi” (I Am That)
and the spiritual path's essence — Advaita (Non-duality),
towards which they both point...

Could it be that modern scientific concepts like Quantum Entanglement and the idea of a
One Mind Universe (or Universal Mind in Singularity)
are also trying to say the same thing? — Dhivo

The spirit of harmony, where the many or even two come together as one —
this is nothing but a Karma Yoga of innovation,
an Advaitic Yajna (non-dual offering)
happening through the principle of proportion... : Dhivo

Some karmas are utterly mad in love with us…
The fruits of selfless actions, born from noble intent,
often take the form of a protective shield —
reaching out to protect us, anytime, anywhere… — Dhivo

People are often seen
compromising their own principles
just to become part of the crowd...
because they fear
the courage it takes to stand alone.

Their survival instinct begins to falter—
and in panic,
they quickly surrender,
falling at anyone's feet
just to feel safe... — Dhivo

Earned a little money and property,

arranged a few comforts for some loved ones—

and people start calling that

"living life"... But in truth,

that's just a well-managed survival.

Living life is the name of an entirely different experience altogether... —Dhivo

---

Educated? Some so-called "well-read" people don't even realize
what they've misunderstood themselves to be...
Truly educated is the one who has mastered the art of choosing the highest values of life. — Dhivo

---

If ever I had to choose between 'pleasure and peace' or 'pain and struggle',
I would undoubtedly choose pain and struggle...
For it is through them that the thirst for Sādhanā (spiritual practice)
and the longing for the Supreme awakens within.
— Dhivo (Dinesh Talekar)

Even if the "Right Time" arrives at the wrong time, we fail to make the most of it. But even if the "Wrong Time" begins at the right time,
we can struggle through it and rise above… — Dhivo (Dinesh Talekar)

"There are BUDDHAs in your time too — those divine souls tirelessly trying to convey the ultimate truth of existence. But the real question is: Are you earnestly trying to receive that greatness? If yes, then Advaita will inevitably unfold..." — Dhivo

---

"It is important to start working on your Aura — to gradually transform it into greater and greater brightness, so that it may ignite your inner spark… and illuminate others too." — Dinesh Talekar (Dhivo)

"**An itinerary of royal legacy begins from your heart**, and because of that, your heart is the ultimate emblem of royalty —
the rest is just an illusion."- Dhivo

Yes, Now and Here — I am the Supreme Greatness...
And simultaneously, I am Simply Nothing.
Yet, I remain on an Eternal Journey towards both,
like a Vega-bond, wandering through the infinite.
— Dhivo

I am always here to guide you — with the teachings of transformation...
But the real question is: Are you on the path? — Dhivo

Life is a flux — a flowing rhythm. If we resist change,
we remain a stagnant pond — never a river,
and far from the Ocean we're meant to become. — Dhivo

"**One of the deepest meanings** of being human is to be a true celebrator of life." - Dhivo

---

When you start treating your problems as projects, your job too transforms into joy — and life becomes lively… more and more lively. : Dhivo

---

To make your vision thrive in the world,
you must learn the art of marketing
and the grace of conscious acting. — Dhivo

Nature holds everything you truly need.
You just have to ask — not from your ego,
but from the depth of your Soul…
and Nature will gently deliver it to you. — DHIVO

Nature can provide you with everything you truly need...
But it suffers deeply when forced to fulfill
what your lust endlessly craves. — Dhivo

A scientist, a philosopher, even an expert — may explain everything about love. But only a true lover can feel it, live it, and be dissolved in it…
so much so, that words disappear,
and silence becomes the only truth. — Dhivo

When inner love begins to overflow outward...
it is not to dominate or dwarf others —
but to gently dissolve, to merge, to become one with them. — Dhivo

---

Fix the goal. Be energetic.
Be focused. Then — walk with persistence.
And keep walking… with unshakable persistence.
One day, you'll turn around and realize —
a miracle has happened within you. — Dhivo

"Right Person, Wrong Path"

- The problem isn't you.

The problem is —
a right person on the wrong path.

So the solution is simple…
Pause. Reflect.
Understand your true path.
The one aligned with your Soul.

And then — walk it.
Lead it with clarity and courage.

What happens next?
Miracles.

Not from outside…
but through you. - Dhivo

Symptoms of the Employee-Minded

- Low energy. Cowardliness. And the habit of backbiting...

These are not just behaviours — they are symptoms. Symptoms of an employee-minded person — someone who has unknowingly surrendered their fire, their freedom, and their vision to comfort, fear, and comparison. - Dhivo

---

Aha! Isn't it truly wonderful?

You just place your mind —
fully, consciously, undivided —
into something…

and it starts to happen.

Slowly, silently,
the universe begins to bend,
time begins to shift,
and life begins to cooperate.

Why?
Because a mind aligned with soul
becomes a magnet for manifestation.

That is the hidden alchemy
of pure attention. - Dhivo

If you ever find yourself tangled in problems or burdened with questions —
Just release them... throw them gently into the vast silence of nature,
or into the sacred intelligence of existence.

You'll be surprised —
how the winds bring whispers of solutions, how the trees echo clarity, how the universe begins to respond in miraculous ways...

Because Nature listens. Existence responds.
But only when you surrender the need to control —
and trust the infinite intelligence of life. — Dhivo

"Love" is the most silvery, goldenised diamond of human existence.
It is not an emotion —
but a luminous frequency that shines through the best in you.

- Explore its infinite horizons.

Dive into it with awe.
Dwell in it like your true home.
Feel it until it dissolves your boundaries.

Merge into it until nothing but love remains.

Because to love is not to possess —
but to become so open,
so present,
so soulfully transparent,
that even the Divine feels welcomed in your being.
— Dhivo

Is It Truly Knowledge, or Just Information?:

- **Are you sure what you've gained is Knowledge?**

Or is it just a decorated accumulation of Information?

Because information can be collected, stored, repeated…

But Knowledge —

- True knowledge is what transforms you.

What humbles you.
What silences your ego and awakens your being.- Dhivo

When Even Death Becomes a Celebration:

- **It's truly beautiful when your life becomes a celebration.**

But it's divinely great when your death becomes one too.

Because to celebrate death is to have lived so consciously,
so fully, so freely —
that even your last breath bows with gratitude. - Dhivo

Selfish or Shellfish — Either Way, You're in a Trap

— Either you are selfish —
chasing your desires like a hungry wolf,

or you are a shellfish —
closed, hiding, afraid to open up.
In both cases, you are trapped.
So wake up.
Rise above both.
And smash the shell of illusion. - Dhivo

Even Animals Are Wondering:

- All animals are silently wondering...

"Here we are, endlessly evolving, struggling to become humans...
and there they are — the humans —

behaving worse than the wildest of us."
How ironic —
the ones who were born at the top
are now falling below the roots. – Dhivo

The Ocean of Failures That Shames Even God:

- What else can one do...

but keep building an ocean of failures,
when every honest effort still ends without success?

Try after try, fall after fall...
and still, no reward.

But if one keeps pouring their soul into the impossible,
with no bitterness, no breaks,

then maybe — just maybe —
not only success, but even God will bow,
feeling ashamed and humbled to bless such a cosmos of determination. - Dhivo

---

The Sacredness of Trying:

In this world, we've been programmed to worship success —
the applause, the numbers, the outcome.

But what if the real temple
is made of wounds, not victories?
Of all those silent, sleepless nights,
Of the broken hopes stitched again,
Of tears wiped by no one but your own courage.
This is not weakness.
This is the making of something divine. - Dhivo
--

The Ocean No One Sees:

No one celebrates your near-wins.
No one claps for your rejections.
No one builds statues for the unseen efforts.

But you know the ocean you're building.
Failure upon failure — not wasted,
but layered like waves rising into a tide.

A tide that one day,
even the stars will recognize. - Dhivo

Why Even the Divine is Moved:

There comes a point when:

Your efforts surpass expectation,

Your resilience surpasses reason,

Your pain transforms into poetry.
And then… something rare happens.

The universe, which had stayed silent,
can no longer ignore you.

Not because you beg.
But because your commitment has become a prayer.

A prayer so vast, so raw, so real —
that even God feels humbled. - Dhivo

So don't stop building that ocean.

Let your failures stack like waves,
not as proof of your defeat,
but as pillars of your becoming.

Because in the end —
success may come. God may descend. Or maybe not.

But you… you will rise as something greater:

Not a winner. Not a loser.
But a warrior of unwavering being.

And even the divine will stand still and whisper —
"This one earned not just success,
but something far rarer — the right to be called sacred." — Dhivo

---

Don't Use Old Answers for New Problems

- If every problem in life appears new —
fresh, unfamiliar, alive —

then why do you still reach
for the same old directions,
worn-out paths,
and borrowed answers? - Dhivo
--

The Death of Inner Intelligence:

We live in a copy-paste culture.

Using recycled wisdom,

Quoting dead philosophers,

Applying outdated solutions
to brand-new dilemmas.

This is not intelligence.
This is intellectual laziness.

It's like wearing winter clothes in summer —
it doesn't just make no sense…
it suffocates your soul.

New Questions Need New Sparks:

Each moment in your life is unrepeatable.
Each challenge is unprecedented.
Each choice is a singular portal.

And still — you bring out
the old map, the old mindset, the old mantras?
That's like trying to navigate the ocean
using a map of the desert.

Make Your Own Path. Spontaneously.:

The rebel yogi doesn't seek answers from others.
He listens to the crisis and creates clarity.

She allows the fire of the problem

to forge her personal response.

Not reaction — but revelation.
Not repetition — but re-imagination.

Because your path must feel born from you,
not borrowed by you.

So the next time you face something confusing, don't rush to quote others. Don't scroll endlessly for advice.
Don't outsource your soul's response.

Instead — Breathe. Stay. Listen. Let something new rise within you.

And if it's raw, uncertain, risky — perfect. Because only real answers feel alive. — Dhivo (Dinesh Talekar)

Wounds Are Wings:

- The greater the struggle,
the louder the criticism,
and the deeper the insult —

the higher will be your flight,
and the grander your success.

--

Pain Is Not the End — It Is the Portal:
Each insult you swallow is not a stone — it's a seed.

Each mocking voice is not your defeat — it's wind beneath your silence. Each time you fall, life isn't pushing you down — it's pulling you deeper, so you can rise wider. > For a bird to soar, it must first battle the storm.

Struggle Carves Out the Space for Grace:
Don't curse your hardships.
Bless them. They are preparing you.
The more intense the fire, the purer the gold.
The more fierce the opposition, the greater the unfolding.

Every tear becomes a torch, if you hold it with awareness.

So if you're being mocked, misunderstood, or minimized — Smile.
Your altitude is being calibrated
by the depth of your pain.
Let your wounds become wings.
Let your silence roar in success.
Because only those who burn,

can one day become the sun. — Dhivo (Dinesh Talekar)

Love Is Not Blind — You Are:

- “Love is blind,” they say —

No, my dear.
It’s not Love that’s blind,
it is lust and possessiveness
that make your eyes go dark.

True Love is not blind —
it is the most conscious alchemy.

What Blinds Us is Not Love:

When you say “Love is blind,”
what you often mean is: “I couldn’t see their flaws.” “I lost myself in them.” “I ignored all the signs.”
But that’s not Love. That’s your attachment wearing perfume.

Lust rushes in. Possessiveness clouds your eyes. Ego pretends it’s forever.
And you call it Love?

Real Love is Radiantly Aware
True Love sees everything.
It doesn't ignore. It doesn't demand. It doesn't bind.
Real Love is alert, awake, and profoundly present.

It allows freedom. It doesn't fear change. It is not afraid of loss.
Because it doesn't cling — it connects.

So next time your heart trembles,
ask yourself: "Am I seeing clearly?"
"Is this Love, or my fear wearing a mask?"
Because when Love truly happens —
you will not lose sight.
You will see more clearly than ever before.
Not with eyes of desire,
but with the vision of the soul. — Dhivo (Dinesh Talekar)

The Difference Between Falling in Love and Rising in Love:

- Most people fall in love… But only a few rise in it. One is driven by gravity of desire, the other — by the levity of awareness.
- ---

Falling is Easy. Rising is Rare.:

To fall in love: Takes no effort. Happens in a moment.
Is mostly emotional and unconscious. Often comes with possession, fear, attachment. It is beautiful — but fragile. Passionate — but reactive. Intense — but often insecure.

And so, many fall. But very few fly.

Rising in Love: A Conscious Climb:
To rise in love is different. It's not a rush. It's a revelation. You rise in love when: You don't need them to complete you.
You're ready to let go if needed. You love them for their being, not for your needs. You grow together, not grasp each other.

Rising in love means evolving through love, not escaping into it.

Love As a Path, Not a Prison Real love is a spiritual path.
It holds your hand not to bind, but to free you from your smaller self.

When two beings rise in love, they don't become dependent —
they become interdependent and divine.

Ask yourself honestly: "Am I falling… or rising?"
Because true love doesn't pull you down. It pulls your soul upward,
towards stillness, strength, and spacious joy.

Fall if you must. But rise — if you truly dare to love. — Dhivo

---

Chaos Is Not in Nature — It's in Your Mind:

The prosperity of nature
is right before your eyes —
flowing in order and simplicity.
But your mind, tangled in chaos,
looks at it with confusion
and turns harmony into disorder.

Nature is Not Complicated — You Are:

The river flows.
The tree grows.
The sun rises without doubt.

No overthinking.
No resistance.
No ego.

Nature lives by truthful rhythm,

but your mind lives in restless friction.

So you miss the beauty,
not because it isn't there —
but because you don't know how to see it. - Dhivo

Complexity is a Man-Made Mirage
You believe:
Simplicity is boring. Silence is emptiness. Order is mechanical.
But this is the illusion of a chaotic mind.

In reality, it's your mental noise
that drowns the song of the birds,
and your expectations
that blur the art of the ordinary. - Dhivo

The Eyes Must Be Quiet:

To experience nature's prosperity,
you don't need effort.

You need stillness.
You need surrender.

A quiet mind is the only eye
that sees the divine precision in wildflowers, and the perfect geometry of a leaf. - Dhivo

---

So next time you feel life is messy,
pause.

Look again — not with thoughts,
but with presence.

You will find that the chaos was never out there.
It was always within.

And when the mind is clear,
even the winds speak in order,
and the rain falls with music. — Dhivo

How to Untangle the Overthinking Mind:

Overthinking is not thinking too much —
it's thinking without awareness.

A tangled mind is not a sign of depth,
but of disconnection from your inner clarity. - Dhivo

Thought Is a Tool, Not a Master:

Your mind is a gift —
a sharp instrument.

But when it runs endlessly,
chasing thoughts like shadows,
it cuts you instead of cutting through illusions.

Overthinking is mental noise
without direction, without grace.

You become busy,
but not wise.
Tired, but not touched by truth. - Dhivo

Why Do We Overthink?
Because we're afraid to feel.
Because we seek control.
Because silence feels like a threat.

The mind races
when the heart is ignored.
You think about life
because you don't know how to be in it. - Dhivo

Three Ways to Untangle the Mind:
1. Pause the Inner Dialogue
You don't always need answers —
sometimes you just need a deep breath.

2. Be Present with Simplicity
Wash a cup, walk barefoot, watch the clouds —

without rushing to interpret.

3. Feel Without Filtering
Let a feeling rise,
without dissecting it.
When you stop interfering,
clarity returns on its own. - Dhivo

You don't need to fight your mind.
Just sit beside it like a loving friend.

Let the thoughts pass.
Let the storm settle.

And when it does,
you'll hear the silence beneath the mind —
the source of your original intelligence. — Dhivo (Dinesh Talekar)

-True intelligence vs borrowed intellect:

No, no, no — stop!
Don't go with them. Those are not intelligent people;
they are just bookish-peckish nerds.

Original intelligence is a totally different phenomenon...

--

Yes, Original Intelligence Is Not Bookish:

Yes, Yes, once again I am repeating..,
No, no, no — stop!
Don't go with them.

They may sound clever,
but they're not truly wise.

They are just bookish-peckish nerds —
chewing on borrowed thoughts,
but starving of real vision.

Books Can Inform You, But Not Transform You

Yes — read. Learn. Study deeply.

But never confuse memory with intelligence. Never mistake data for depth.

They quote others, but they have no voice of their own.

They carry facts, but not the fire.

What Is Original Intelligence?

Original intelligence is raw. It arises from presence, not from the pages.

It is the spark that questions — the light that sees without bias. It is not “taught” — it is touched within.

True Intelligence Feels Like This:

A sudden silence in the mind. A clarity that doesn't need debate.

A knowing that has no reference, yet feels complete.

It’s when you dare to see freshly, think differently, and act without approval.

It’s the rebel’s intelligence — born in solitude, and sculpted by experience.

Don’t just become a walking library. Be a living flame.

Because wisdom isn't printed — it's breathed.

And if the whole world quotes others,
let you become the one who gets quoted. — Dhivo
(Dinesh Talekar)

Wake Up! Your Life Is Not Yet Lived:

Look at yourself —
your life is just a hypnotized sleep,
and your sleep is a delusive chaos.
You're not living,
you're just drifting.

You eat, you work, you laugh, you suffer…
But where is the awakened spark in all of it?

Where is the touch of presence? - Dhivo

The Sleep You Call Life:

This hypnotic life:

Is full of noise, but no melody

Is full of movement, but no meaning
Is driven by patterns, not purpose

You are asleep, not just in bed —
but even while walking, working, praying.

Even your dreams are not yours —
they are borrowed from society, culture, and fear. - Dhivo

But Awakening Changes Everything:

When the spirit awakens,
even ordinary breath becomes extraordinary.

Life becomes a conscious celebration

Sleep becomes a canvas of divine imagination
Your emotions stop enslaving you — they start serving creativity.
Your mind doesn't chatter — it starts composing.

The chaos transforms into cosmic music.
You no longer sleep like a victim —
you rest like a god dreaming creation. - Dhivo

So ask yourself, now —

Am I awake? Or just reacting in a dream-like habit?

Because the moment you awaken, Life stops being survival...
and becomes a sacred dance of awareness. — Dhivo (Dinesh Talekar)

You are the route to your own root —
to rise and ripen as the fruit. — Dhivo

The most serious problem with the modern generation is "self-talk-lessness."
So first, learn, how to talk with yourself,
face to face... — Dhivo

Supreme success is a two-way blossoming —
like a tree that grows deep with roots,
and rises prosperously with
branches, leaves, seeds, flowers, and fruits. — Dhivo

Actually, success is just a hallucination —

a spark to awaken your spirit and lead you forward.
The real achievements lie within the journey itself: in experiencing, knowing, feeling, understanding, learning — and much more. — Dhivo

---

When you look deeply at your Master,
you feel his inner spirit has overflowed outward —
just to show you a bright path of glory. — Dhivo

Beware of mere outer success — it often comes wrapped in ego, lust, and inner blindness. — Dhivo

---

And he who knows the truth of the Self and the Supreme — through direct experience —
may indeed be dwelling in the realm of the Buddha. — Dhivo

Look deep into the ocean of life —
you are not here merely for happiness and joy;
those are just by-products.
You are the chosen one by Existence
for its ultimate task.
Understand it... and perform it. — Dhivo

Failures are the robust foundation of supreme success. — Dhivo

---

'Only success' is just the intriguing jugglery of life;
but success after failures —
that is the ecstasy of supremacy. — Dhivo

Oh Human!
The vision in your eyes,
the charm and glow on your face,
and the radiant aura of your being —
these are what truly set you apart from animals. — Dhivo

Success is the ultimate lotus —
risen from the innermost quagmire of your failures.
— Dhivo

He who only knows the knowledge, but not by experience —
may merely be a philosopher. — Dhivo

People are always saying one thing,
thinking another,
and understanding something else entirely.

Because the very nature of people —
of the crowd, of the group —
is chaos.

Truth belongs only to the individual.
So speak as an individual,
think and understand as an individual —
not as a crowd, not as a group,
but as a conscious human being. — Dhivo

If you are only constructing on the outside,
then all your high-profile societies, bungalows, and villas
are nothing but hollow graves in disguise.

And ultimately,
your permanent residence will be —
a cemetery... a graveyard. — Dhivo

Jesus said,
"Let the dead bury their dead — you, come with me."

But we, the hypnotized animals,
are still crawling

on the dead, lecherous path... — Dhivo

Yes — die to the past,
because it is only Now and Here
that you are truly alive. — Dhivo

Are you truly in need of marriage?
If yes, then go ahead — be married.

But remember:
Marriage means merging —
one dissolves into one,
until, by and by,
there remains no two... only One,
and eventually, simply None. — Dhivo

Do or die — but from now on,
be nothing less than a businessman,
yes — an entrepreneur.
An employee? Never.

I'm not speaking of employees or employers —
I'm pointing toward the entrepreneur within you,
the leader inside you
waiting to rise. — Dhivo

Success is a beautiful nightmare...
but still, a nightmare.

Only the journey is real —
a living, breathing,
blossoming journey. — Dhivo

Actually,
there is no need to run at all.

But you,
foolish creatures,
keep running —
for prestige, power, and luxury.

And still,
if you must run —
then run for the ultimate concern. — Dhivo

Acceptance of life in its totality,
and surrender to it with your whole being —
this is the true realm of Femininity. — Dhivo

Arise, run, and achieve your goal
by awakening the leader within you —
and in doing so,
prove your true masculinity. — Dhivo

The last obstacle between you and success
is not fate, not failure —
it is languor. — Dhivo

Beware of the so-called politicians, film-stars, and novelists —
they are often leading you toward a dead life.

Instead,
be aware of your own being,
your inner vision,
and lead yourself
toward a humanely alive life. — Dhivo

Don't deceive yourself.
Don't float the hoax that you are human.

If you truly are — then go,
do something creative, generous, and deeply humane. — Dhivo

Don't blame others. You are the main obstacle in your own life.

Just step aside, and let life flow its own way — like a river. — Dhivo

---

The most dangerous contemporary disease infecting today's youth is —
"Time Pass." — Dhivo

It's urgent!
Remove the word "Time Pass" from your dictionary —
otherwise,
it will remove you from your life's very territory.— Dhivo

Hey! You all Youngsters — stop right where you are...
Break your sleep. Know yourself.
And arise as a visionary, great spirit
this world is waiting for. — Dhivo

Don't be deceived by the fake glamour of so-called politics, films, and novels.

Instead, be the one to create visionary politics, creative films, and mature, truth-filled novels. — Dhivo

---

In the truest sense,
there is no fixed law for life —
not for anything.

The moment you try to make a law,
it becomes false — an untruth.

Maybe… yes, maybe,
there is only one law —
the law of CHANGE —
a constant, ever-unfolding change. — Dhivo

"The Lost Child Within" - dhivo

I do not wish to become a so-called politician, chairman, or any kind of famous or powerful personality.
Rather, I long to remain a simple, ordinary human being —
one who can laugh loudly, love lordly, share purely, care consciously, and play plentifully…

But alas, our so-called society, with all its status and labels, never allows us to resurrect as a child again.

And yet, Jesus says,
"Only children can enter into my God's Paradise."

Our so-called society, with all its status and labels, will never allow us to resurrect as a child again...

And yet, Jesus says: "Only children can enter into my God's Paradise." — Dhivo

---

"The courage to stand alone against all odds — That is the true realm of Soldier-hood." — Dhivo

The Inner Warrior:

In a world where blending in feels safe, and standing up invites isolation, true inner warriors are forged — not by might, but by unwavering spirit. Soldierhood is not about battles outside, but bravery within: the bravery to face your truth, break your conditioning, and walk alone — when needed — towards what's right, not what's easy.

Spiritual Soldierhood:

A spiritual soldier doesn't carry weapons —
He carries awareness.
He doesn't fight people —

He wages war against ignorance, injustice, and the inner sleep.

He doesn't kill —
He destroys illusions.
He doesn't conquer lands —
He conquers himself.

His battlefield is silence.
His victory is compassion.
His discipline is not from fear,
But from love for truth.

Even if the whole world mocks him,
He walks his path —
With wounds of truth on his chest,
And the light of knowing in his eyes.

He is not here to please.
He is not here to impress.
He is here to awaken.
And sometimes that means — standing alone,
Calm in chaos,
Clear in confusion,
A rebel wrapped in divine fire.
This is Spiritual Soldierhood —
Not a posture of pride,
But the posture of presence. — Dhivo

"Your eyes can only see... but your vision — it is the sea." — Dhivo

Your eyes can only see... but your vision — it is the sea.
Not just the surface, but the depths of truth it can feel.
Eyes capture the form, but vision holds the formless,
It dives into the unknown, where the spirit becomes fearless.
So, close your mere sight — and awaken the seeing within.
There… lies the ocean where your true journey begins. — Dhivo

---

The whole of Nature is your Kingdom,
and you are the King of your own Life.
A Kingship is not a position —
it is an attitude towards Life.
An inner stance of awareness,
responsibility, and grace. — Dhivo (Dinesh D. Talekar)

Your greatness may be defined by your vision for life,

but your success is defined by your courage to run towards that vision... — Dhivo

---

Strength is powerless without a powerful vision, and vision is blind without the strength to live it... — Dhivo

---

We cannot learn everything from the experiences of others.
Some experiences are so ultimate,
that we must—absolutely must—dwell into them ourselves,
to truly learn the realm they hold within... — Dhivo

Yes, eyes are two, but Vision is only one...
So, align both your eyes toward your ultimate vision — Focus. Lead it. Live it. Achieve it. — Dhivo

---

What a wonderful message it is:
"Be open and natural — and it will happen to you..."— Dhivo

The ecstasy of celebration lies in the ultimate union —
of Life and Death,
of Love and Hate,
of Joy and Sorrow...
and the endless dance of opposites in harmony. — Dhivo

Every solution in life lies within.
We just need to awaken the inner conscience and listen deeply to the voice of intuition. — Dhivo

---

Rebel!
Rebel against the pseudo happiness, against the comfort of laziness,
and the mask of a fake personality...

Only then shall you truly conquer
the inner enemies —

the lack of awareness, the whispering ego,
the storms of hatred,
the flames of anger,
and the seductive illusions of lust for life. — Dhivo

Your cleverness, scholarliness, and smartness— they are but tiny particles, mere specs of your Intellectual Quotient...

But the real atoms—
are the irrational rationality
and the illogical logic
that defy convention and yet reveal the unseen truth. — Dhivo

---

Find your original being.
What you think of yourself is merely an amalgamation of habits, patterns, and past conditioning.
But your real nature —
is an entirely different phenomenon,
silent, vast, and untouched by borrowed identities.
— Dhivo

You cannot find me as a 'crowd',
for now I am completely alone —
but remember, not lonely…
Aloneness is my strength,
not my absence. — Dhivo

Live in solitude.

Be alone.
Only then will you begin to feel
the gravity of true awareness—
the silent weight of your own presence. — Dhivo

'Rebellious Flower'
is like a fiery SUN within
and a glorious MOON in vision... — Dhivo

Look at the white cloud,
look at the flower,
look at the river…
and finally, look within—you.— Dhivo

Oh Dear Leader,
If you are not capable of inspiring millions of lives,
then your own life is nothing more than a hollow bamboo... — Dhivo

---

Truth is a definition-less particle,
a spontaneous action,
the right and total acceptance of what is... — Dhivo

Your whole life is crawling toward death, right before your eyes —
yet you continue to behave like a hypnotized, addicted creature... — Dhivo

---

There's no such thing as wrong English or wrong language—
but yes, wrong communication can lead you into deep misery.
So forget everything else,
and just learn to communicate rightly... — Dhivo

"Sands of Time, Played by Giants with Childish Minds":

Politicians, business tycoons, and celebrities are not merely gambling with their own lives—
but with the lives of many others,
all for power, prestige, and wealth.
They are like small children
playing on the sands of time... — Dhivo

"Clinging to life means death will cling to you.
And chasing happiness, wealth, or fame

is merely running toward misery, poverty, and shame—
because whatever the mind craves is bound to the law of duality.” — Dhivo

in a nutshell, “Run behind happiness, and misery follows.
Crave life too tightly, and death clings tighter. Whatever the mind desires lives in duality.” — Dhivo

---

“Existence has its own timetable —
just wait, watch,
and align yourself with deeper intelligence.
Try not harder, but smarter.” — Dhivo

"Conscious rebelliousness is always positive —
it sets you apart from the crowd,
not in arrogance, but in awakened authenticity." — Dhivo

"When every moment of your life becomes an uncertain adventure for you,
and a headline-worthy wonder for others —
then simply, this is 'the life'." — Dhivo

"If you feel me consciously,

you'll realize —
love is not madness,
it is supreme ecstasy."— Dhivo

"Creativity is a spontaneous action born in complete relaxation —
or simply, it is the natural way of life." — Dhivo

"The journey of life is nothing but the art of balancing with Existence —
a harmonious dance between the spiritual, mental, and physical realms." — Dhivo

---

Come on, dear —
Let's have some fun,
Let's fall in love…
We are not programmed machines. — Dhivo

Literally, we ruin our present—
either by clinging to old memories
or by dreaming in hallucinations. — Dhivo

Only an uncertain and unsecured life is truly

alive; everything else is merely a living death... — Dhivo

Life is all about happening, not about doing...
Life is all about spontaneous action, not about pre-planned activity... — Dhivo

---

Existence seeks your response, not your reaction —
because only response can truly prosper life... — Dhivo

Go deep within,
dive into the ocean of your own being,
and resurrect the sacred enigma of your originality... — Dhivo

---

Get out of your home —
only the weak perish in comfort,
but warriors are born and remembered on the battlefield... — Dhivo

---

Definitely, you are born with something special —

you just have to recognize it and let it shine. — Dhivo

A golden spoon is a curse,
but struggle — the greatest blessing —
that shapes the true realm of life. — Dhivo

Once ears said to me, " We twins are born to listen the Music, Melody and Mantra"...:

Science says, "Neurons that fire together, wire together."
So, sit silently beneath a banyan tree…
Let your senses dissolve into the symphony of nature —
The gentle chirping of birds,
The blossoming of fruits and flowers,
The soft whispers of leaves, branches, and the wind,
The rhythmic fall of waterfalls and raindrops…
Or simply lose yourself in the soothing notes of a flute
or the embrace of divine music.
Let such moments fire your neurons —
not with noise, but with melodious stillness... — Dhivo

Short Film Title: **Who is the Police?**
Writer: Dhivo (Dinesh Dilip Talekar)
Scene Opens:
Four traffic police officers are back again for checking at University Square after several days. They stand around, looking here and there, chatting among themselves.

One of them blows the whistle, signalling vehicles to stop.
The orange light switches to red now.
The traffic from one side begins to halt.

The whistling officer now halts the traffic on this side and signals vehicles from the other side to proceed. He moves to the center of the intersection to help control the remaining traffic.

The other three officers approach the stopped vehicles and begin inspecting suspiciously, as if searching for a criminal. They start randomly checking people.

Just then, the hero and his friend also arrive on their two-wheeler, Chetak, and stop at the signal. Seeing the police checking so thoroughly, they feel slightly nervous.

To be continued...

One officer demands money.
The hero pulls out □500 and hands it over.
Then he begins emptying his pockets, giving whatever he has to the officer.
Next, he takes off his shirt and places it in the officer's hand.
The officer shouts, "What are you doing?"

The hero begins unbuckling his belt and says—
“Sir, □500 isn’t enough for you anyway... you won't stop there. If it came to that, you’d want even our skin along with our clothes.”

"Sir, you’re taking money—
but along with it, you’re also taking the curse and grief of my family.”

Suddenly, the officer is reminded of something at home (Flashback):
He walks into his house and sees his son drinking alcohol and smoking with friends, completely intoxicated.
In anger, he grabs his son by the collar and yells—
“You’ll drink yourself to death one day!”

(Back to the present scene)

The hero echoes the same words:

"You carry home not just the bribe—but also curses...
Children will go astray, they'll drink, and smoke...
and the curse of corruption will show its consequences, one way or another..."

To be continued...

The hero raises his hand, as if to strike the officer.

The officer barks, "You dare raise your hand on a cop, you scoundrel?!"

The hero replies with fiery calm:
"I could never even think of raising a hand against the police.
But if a scoundrel in uniform asks for a bribe from a common man—
I will still protect the dignity of that uniform.
I won't let the uniform be disgraced!"

And with that, the hand raised in anger transforms into a clenched fist, a declaration.

He shouts aloud: "Bharat Mata Ki..."
Some bystanders at the signal, still stuck in traffic, respond with "Jai!"

The officers step back, now visibly unsettled.

The hero shouts again, louder: "Bharat Mata Ki..."
The crowd replies, this time more united: “Jai!”
Many raise their fists into the air in solidarity.

Then the hero raises his hand again and says—
“Sadrakshanaya...”
(Some people respond) “...Khalnigrahanaya!”

He repeats louder, looking straight into the officer’s eyes, hand raised:
“Sadrakshanaya...”
The crowd roars back:
“Khalnigrahanaya!”

Narration continues:

To become a true police officer, a uniform alone isn’t enough...
Honesty is equally essential.

The one who protects the good and disciplines the wicked—that is the true police.
Even common citizens can be protectors of the system...
If only they understand this sacred mantra of democracy—
“Sadrakshanaya Khalnigrahanaya.”

The constable, moved and ashamed, nods his head and steps back.
He pulls out the □500 bribe from his pocket and returns it to the hero.

\---

The hero, emotional now, says—

“If I’ve made a mistake, then fine me fairly,
but don’t make finding faults a daily ritual just to pocket money.
Taking bribes isn’t just corruption...
It’s a demonic conspiracy to hollow out our nation’s economic and social roots from within.”

\---

To be continued...

\---

Disclaimer:
This short film is a work of fiction.
The characters, events, and settings depicted in the film are purely fictional, and any resemblance to actual persons, living or dead, or to actual events or locales is entirely coincidental. The views and opinions expressed are those of the characters and do not necessarily reflect those of the filmmakers or any affiliated entities.
Viewer discretion is advised.

Right Desire, Right Willpower, and Right Action —

this is the true formula for Achievement. — Dhivo

Desire alone is utterly impotent.
It needs the strength of Willpower and the fire of Action
to be fulfilled. — Dhivo

What is wrong with today's youth?
Education, job, marriage, and then children —
Is this what you call a "settled life"? — Dhivo

Do or die,
but never compromise with your vision.
Otherwise, your life will become
a body without a soul... — Dhivo

Find your "Passion for Life" — and find it now.
Otherwise, you will merely remain an animal…
an unborn human being. — Dhivo

Your boredom is nothing but the absence of a true passion for life...— Dhivo

---

Lack of awareness gives birth to misunderstanding,
which grows into misconception—
and that misconception gives rise to anger, hatred, lust, and ego.
All of these become the breeding ground of deathlike misery...

So, Meditate...
Contemplate...
And only then, Act—
For this is how one creates a divine life. — Dhivo

Go deep into Life…
Penetrate it with total strength and sincerity…
Then, Resurrection shall happen to you —
A brand new, second birth…
The 'Dwij', as the ancient ones called it. – Dhivo

Somewhere along the way,
I found that life is a kind of serious joke...
But when seen from a higher vantage point,
in the Now and Here —
Life reveals itself as

a purely divine happening. — Dhivo

A man of higher values,
vision, and awakened thoughts
is the true emperor —
ruling not over lands,
but over infinite hearts. — Dhivo

One of the most dangerous yet precious possessions —
Your Ego.
Don't let it roam freely,
Lock it deep within,
and keep it sealed…
for life. — Dhivo

Sometimes, it seems as if love begins from the body and travels towards the soul...
But in truth,
Love arises from the Infinite Unknown —
and dissolves back into the same silence... — Dhivo

--

At times, it feels like love starts from the body and flows toward the soul...
But truly, Love is a whisper from the Infinite Unknown —
A cosmic spark that visits you for a while, only to merge again into the great Mystery… — Dhivo

--

They told you —
Love begins with the body and climbs toward the soul...
But the truth is far more rebellious —
Love descends from the Unknown,
not to make you whole,
but to shatter your false wholeness…
It is not a journey from touch to soul,
It is a storm that starts beyond the stars
and leaves you naked —
Raw, surrendered, and Infinite. — Dhivo

It's rare to find real youth around here—
Because our mental software is so outdated...
It skips the vibrant fire of youth
and leaps straight from childish ignorance
to a frozen, fake maturity of the old.
What a tragedy—
The rebel flame dies before it even learns to burn.
— Dhivo

Great alchemies happen
when two opposites dare to merge—
in the presence of the Supreme Divine...
It is the friction of contrast that gives birth to transformation.

Yes, even two similar beings may unite—
but seldom do they dissolve into non-duality.
Without the challenge of difference,
there's little fuel for transcendence. — Dhivo

Sacrifice, Compromise, and Adjustment—
these are the robust backbones
of all meaningful human relations…
and gradually, they become the very spine of life itself. — Dhivo

---

The true identity of a 'Human Being'
is not in his name or status,
but in the depth of his
Love, Sacrifice, and Generosity. — Dhivo

The most dangerous disease of the human mind
is not hatred or fear—
it is Misunderstanding...
And its root cause is simply one thing:
Unconsciousness. — Dhivo

Feeding information from the outside,
without ever touching the inner core of a student—
this is the tragic reality
of our so-called educational universities. — Dhivo

The true meaning of Education
is not to stuff the mind,
but to draw out the hidden talent—
to awaken the inner knowing
from the disciple's very core. — Dhivo

The one who teaches his students
to deny blindly, to doubt deeply,
and to question courageously—
he alone is the original teacher. — Dhivo

There is a sacred art to giving a solution —
First, listen with presence,

then understand with empathy,
analyze with awareness,
and only then resolve with wisdom...
But sadly, many self-proclaimed counselors
are just chatterboxes echoing their own noise. — Dhivo

I truly appreciated the concept — "Think and Grow Rich,"
but in living it, I discovered a deeper truth:
"Think, Implement, and Grow Richer Within."
Because the eternal wealth lies not in possession,
but in inner transformation. — Dhivo

There is nothing more powerful
than the heart of a voluntary sacrificer —
for it bleeds not in weakness,
but blossoms in silent strength... — Dhivo

It's not about success, fame, or fleeting opportunities...
It's about your alive response —
your conscious pulse echoing back to Life itself. — Dhivo

I’m not sure if I possess the 7 habits of highly influential people,
but one thing I know for sure —
Thinking is my favourite habit. — Dhivo

The most neglected topics in human society are sex and death, as well as sleep and dreams.
No one dares to discuss them openly...
But if one dares to contemplate upon these,
the hidden doors of existence
shall surely begin to open. — Dhivo

Paradoxical, yet true:
Escapists are the real sinners...
So enter deep into life,
crack through sorrow, pain, and struggle —
for this is the only path
towards true holiness. — Dhivo

Life exists between two opposites,
and balancing in between them
is the scientific art of truly alive living... — Dhivo

When your wavelength of “sense of humor”
resonates with someone’s heart and intellect,

an ego-less friendship begins to blossom from within... — Dhivo

---

Beware of the so-called clever businessmen—
they will either convince you or confuse you,
only to use you for their mortal trivialities... — Dhivo

There is no such thing as Bad, Sorrow, or Hell in Life —
It's simply the absence of the Best, Happiness, and the Heavenly... — Dhivo

---

First, we must accept the reality.
Then, we must raise the right questions.
And only after that, unite and ignite
for the real solutions that lead
to the true realm of life... — Dhivo

What Dhivo Yoga – Meditation & Spirituality Center truly understands, knows, and believes about immortal work is this:

To create a wave of consciousness
and to empower souls with the higher values of life,
echoing across hearts and cultures—
awakening the world from within. — Dhivo

When you focus, concentrate, and pour your wholehearted attention into one ultimate seed — a higher task, project, or purpose —
it is destined to blossom into a grand golden tree of success... — Dhivo

---

Everything here is constantly moving and changing...
So how can one rigidly define the "purpose" of life?
But yes — one can celebrate, serve, and transform this very life towards the higher and the ultimate...
— Dhivo

In my experienced reflection,
the desire for enlightenment

may be the last barrier to enlightenment itself... — Dhivo

You cannot skip the struggles and hurdles of your own life.
You must pass through them —
penetrate them deeply — to resurrect as your original being... — Dhivo

---

Becoming rich or prosperous is merely a by-product.
As you choose richer and higher words,
your thinking transforms,
and soon your actions and atmosphere
begin to reflect that richness... — Dhivo

Relax...
Search within for your true potential.
Think deeply, pick the best idea, test it.
If it resonates with your passion,
then lead it with persistence—
like a determined marathon racer... — Dhivo

You are always eligible,
always on time,
forever young —

to do new things,
to dream new dreams,
to live a new life… — Dhivo

There are five profound milestones
on the unknown path of spiritual search.
At each, you must surrender what feels most precious — when the time comes...

- Leave your outer desires
- Leave your people
- Leave even your master
- Leave your ultimate concern
- And finally, leave yourself…

Only then, the unknown reveals itself. — Dhivo

I have no rigid goal to achieve,
but an alive path to walk, to breathe, to lead... — Dhivo

There's nothing truly wrong
in doing what others call "wrong" —
if your intention is pure
and your behaviour remains humane… — Dhivo

I do not side with mere smart work,
nor do I blindly favour hard work…

My way is the sacred balance —
of intellectual sharpness
and devotional persistence.

First, think like a sage,
then work like a warrior. — Dhivo

Alert to the Youth!
You are getting hypnotized — trapped by the glittering cage of MNCs and corporates.
10-hour shifts, night duties, robotic chaos...
And in return?
They lure you into a hollow, overpriced lifestyle —
multiplexes, shopping malls, pubs and restaurants,
branded illusions, fast food addictions,
and the fake glow of show-off culture.

Wake up before you become just another product in their system.
Reclaim your time, your mind, your being. — Dhivo

"Life is newness, unknownness, and spontaneous flow, simply, a ceaseless flux of unending variety." — Dhivo

Observe again, "Life is a spontaneous dance of the unknown —
forever fresh, ever-changing, endlessly diverse." - Dhivo

"Karma is an inevitable phenomenon in life —
but what truly matters is your conscious choice
and your intention aligned with higher values." — Dhivo

Listen again, "Karma is bound to happen,
but when chosen with awareness and rooted in higher values,
it becomes the path to liberation." – Dhivo

"The most urgent need of humanity is to place meditation before education — otherwise, these chaotic educational systems may one day lead human machines into the final world war."— Dhivo

think again, "Meditation must precede education —
for without inner clarity,
today's education may program tomorrow's destruction." – Dhivo

---

“Raising human consciousness to its higher potential
is one of the most righteous and balanced acts
of social work — whether as a social worker or a spiritual leader.” — Dhivo

---

"Perhaps, Yog is not truly for physical or psychological fitness — that’s merely a byproduct phenomenon.
In my understanding, Yog is a scientific spiritual method — an inner itinerary to lead one's being toward the Unknown Divine." — Dhivo

---

When you find yourself
trapped in a chaotic crowd,
you begin to realize
the true importance of solitude.

And when you feel
depressed in loneliness,
you begin to understand
the true value of togetherness... — Dhivo

Imagination is the
soul of knowledge —
it aligns and harmonizes

information, experimentation,
and experience. — Dhivo

Humanity is nothing but
a conscious and spontaneous
act of generosity. — Dhivo

There are countless ways
to earn a billion dollars,
but the true quest is
to discover the way
to awaken a billion-dollar
humane vision... — Dhivo

Nothing is small
or less significant —
every single feather matters
in crafting the wings
of your grand success. — Dhivo

'Understanding'
is the true earning of life —
it alone can lead us
into the realm of
nothingness, somethingness,
or perhaps… everything,

even beyond death. — Dhivo

If one truly decides from the core —

from the burning fire of the solar plexus,

the Manipur Chakra, then earning a billion dollars is not impossible...

But to attain a billion-dollar humane vision; that is rare, that is divine. — Dhivo

---

Swami Vivekananda is not just a name —
He is the emblem of the real youth dwelling within you.
He is the divine nectar, potent enough to dissolve every layer
of your false personality.
He is the infinite spirit of awakened youngness,
born to ignite the hidden Vivekananda within you.
— Dhivo

"Humane intention is the sacred key

that unlocks the true path of Karma Yoga." — Dhivo

"One of the greatest reasons to be grateful
is the sheer miracle that
—we are alive, and we know it.
We are not just breathing,
we are aware that we are breathing.
That conscious aliveness
is the deepest ground of gratitude." — Dhivo

To begin with, come...
Let's fill ourselves with compassion,
with a sense of gratitude so deep—
that meditation begins to happen
on its own...
in its own rhythm,
in its own sacred time. - Dhivo

Yogic Pain is a Holistic Medicine.
Understand this—not just intellectually,
but from the deepest bottom of your brain.

Now stretch, twist, mold, and bend

your body with a conscious grace—
from the root of your navel
while feeling it resonate
at the sacred depth of your heart.

For in this pain lies the alchemy
of healing, wholeness, and awakening. – Dhivo

Why do we breathe, digest, and sleep on autopilot mode?
Who is behind such consciously subconscious actions?
Do the right questions matter—
or can even stupid questions become game changers?
What do you think? - Dhivo
--

Rethink, Why do we breathe, digest, and sleep on autopilot?
Who is orchestrating these deeply intelligent actions
when we are not even trying?

Is it the subconscious?
Or is it the supreme conscious playing silently behind the curtain?
The question burns...

But remember— It's not always about asking right questions.
Sometimes, even a so-called stupid question can open the gates to a deeper revolution. Because it's not the question,
but the quest behind it that matters. - Dhivo

Zen, Ikigai, Hara, Tanden, and Haiku —
these are some of the finest spiritual gems to imbibe from the sacred land of Japan. – Dhivo

---

"Right Intention" by Dhivo

"Right Intention" is a
costly personal affair.
We can't expect it from all—
only a rare few
can attain this milestone
of a truly humane life.

But to convey it rightly,
one must be in tune with
timing, perspective,
and conscious action. — Dhivo

A Yoga Instructor or even a Gym Trainer
may be able to open the door to "Yoga",
but only a humane intention
holds the true key
to unlock the sacred path of "Yog". — Dhivo

"Materialistic achievement" may be the foundation of your so-called success in life, but in reality,
it's just a game of hormones for your mind,
and a drama of time for your soul... — Dhivo
Dhivo Yoga Meditation Wellness Center

It seems that "Misunderstanding"
is the surface-level foundation of Sansara (the worldly entanglement),
but deep beneath,
it is "Dharana" — the fixed inner perception — that silently fuels every action, ultimately weaving the illusion of "Prapanch" (the projected world)...— Dhivo

---

"Cunningness"
is a twisted concoction
brewed from ego, jealousy, and hatred,

flavored secretly with
selfishness, lust, and at times, cruelty...
In essence,
it's nothing but a boomerang of curse
returning to its origin. - Dhivo

Sometimes, even exaggeration
becomes a necessity — when reluctance
chokes the guts of a whistleblower.—Dhivo

A family man's heart once said, "Believe in me... If needed, I will sow myself into the soil—and resurrect as a mango tree for you." — Dhivo

---

Come! Let's walk
into the Woods of Universally Humane Spirituality...
to awaken, to expand,
to grow within—
the sacred capacity to simply be. — Dhivo

Be a Humane Magnet
In this inward journey,
a magnet attracts magnet—
not iron.

But even iron, through inner alchemy,
can transform into a super magnet... — Dhivo

...And the one who truly understands
the profound essence of "enjoying life"—
through exploration, experiments, and experiences—
is the one who is transforming potential into a real human being. — Dhivo

---

Observer — The Way of Being Conscious
"Drashtā Bhāva", the state of pure witnessing,
is not about what is seen,
but about what you are capable of seeing...
It's not the object,
but your awakened perception
that defines the depth of observation. — Dhivo

"**...And the fruits are merely a by-product** at the far end of the Tree of Life —
what truly matters are the roots." — Dhivo

--

Listen again, …And the fruits — they are but a passing sweetness,

a by-product blooming at the far end of the Tree of Life.
What truly nourishes, what truly anchors,
are the invisible roots beneath —
silent, unseen, yet sacred.

The depth determines the height.
The inner holds the outer.
And life, like a tree, stands firm
only if its roots touch something eternal..." — Dhivo

"In this chaotic contemporary world,
what we truly need — more than love or brotherhood — is Humane Friendship...
A friendship rooted in understanding,
free from possession,
and flowing with presence..." — Dhivo

"A deeper dimension of understanding
is not just to know or agree—
but to truly accept and honor the diverse forms and frequencies in which understanding itself appears..." — Dhivo

---

"If only they could drink
their own inhumane behaviour,
their entire being would want to
vomit it out from the depths
of their soul..." — Dhivo

"A humane warrior enters the war—
not out of revenge,
but for the sake of compassion,
duty, and justice..." — Dhivo

"When abstract logic transforms into humane devotion,
it opens the doorway to the divine unknown.
Just like a caterpillar becoming a butterfly
opens the skies of its innate flight..." — Dhivo

Only knowing is not enough —
one must perform the higher values of Life.
Togetherness holds deep importance,
but it becomes truly powerful
only when it happens at the right time..." — Dhivo

"Giving each other time at the right time
is also one of the highest values of life..."

Togetherness is the key to fulfilling the purpose of life...:Dhivo

---

The dictionary of a "Humane Warrior"
does not contain the word Revenge,
but rather—Duty, Compassion,
Forgiveness, and even Respect.
To enter a war or conflict, then,
is not out of rage, but as a duty
born from deep compassion...— Dhivo

From the vantage point of Non-Duality,
Detachment is a deeply humane understanding.
It has nothing to do with avoiding, distancing,
or separation.
It is like a lotus in the mud —
connected yet untouched,
attached yet detached. — Dhivo

While dwelling in the material realm,
Detachment becomes a highly relative phenomenon,
deeply intertwined with the humane understanding of connection, separation, escape, and surrender. — Dhivo

---

It is shallow to judge or label someone
merely by observing their parrot-like knowledge or even sharp intelligence.
What truly matters—what changes the game on both sides—is their Humane Intention. — Dhivo

---

One of the greatest reasons

to be grateful and to express gratitude
is the simple yet profound truth:
We are alive — and we are aware of it.
We are truly alive... — Dhivo

Why is it necessary to meditate?
There are many reasons...
But to begin with, let's start with something simple: bathing.

Yes, why do we bathe?
To clean our body.
We bathe every day, sometimes even twice a day.
And then?
We decorate the body with our choicest clothes.

What next?
We go to work, to a party, or somewhere else...

Likewise, meditation is a kind of bathing —
but for the mind.

A kind of sun-bathing for the soul.
Just as we expose the body to sunlight to absorb vital rays,
so too in meditation, we expose our inner world to awareness.

Even animals bask in the sun
—to clean their bodies,
to rid their fur of parasites.

In the same way, in meditation,
we observe our body,
our breath,
our thoughts,
and most importantly —
our mind.

We cleanse it.
We purify it.
Because, as the theory of relativity in quantum physics suggests:

- "The observer affects the observed."

And then — it is up to you what you do

with this newly cleansed and awakened psycho-somatic being:
your mind-body-energy system.

You can channel it into Karma Yoga,
into Sadhana Yoga,
or even misuse it toward destruction.

But...
it becomes extremely difficult to walk an inhumane path
once you have dwelled deeply
in the pond of Dhyan – Dharana – Sadhana.

So, a regular cleansing —
of yourself,
and your inner tools: mind, body, and energy —
can lead you towards the realm of life.

And in time...
another hidden door may open —
a door leading you toward the Divine Unknown,
as you evolve within it.

— Dhivo, YouTube.com/DhivoYoga

If one truly wishes to feel the planet earth...
Then rise early in the morning,
And run into the woods –
Into nature, into solitude... – Dhivo

Come! Let’s walk together on the path of understanding..; Dhivo
Youtube.com/DhivoYoga | Youtube.com/Dhivo | Dhivo.in Facebook.com/DineshTalekarDhivo | Facebook.com/MeditativeYoga
Free Courses: Udemy.com/Heart-Meditation | Udemy.com/WorkingYogi

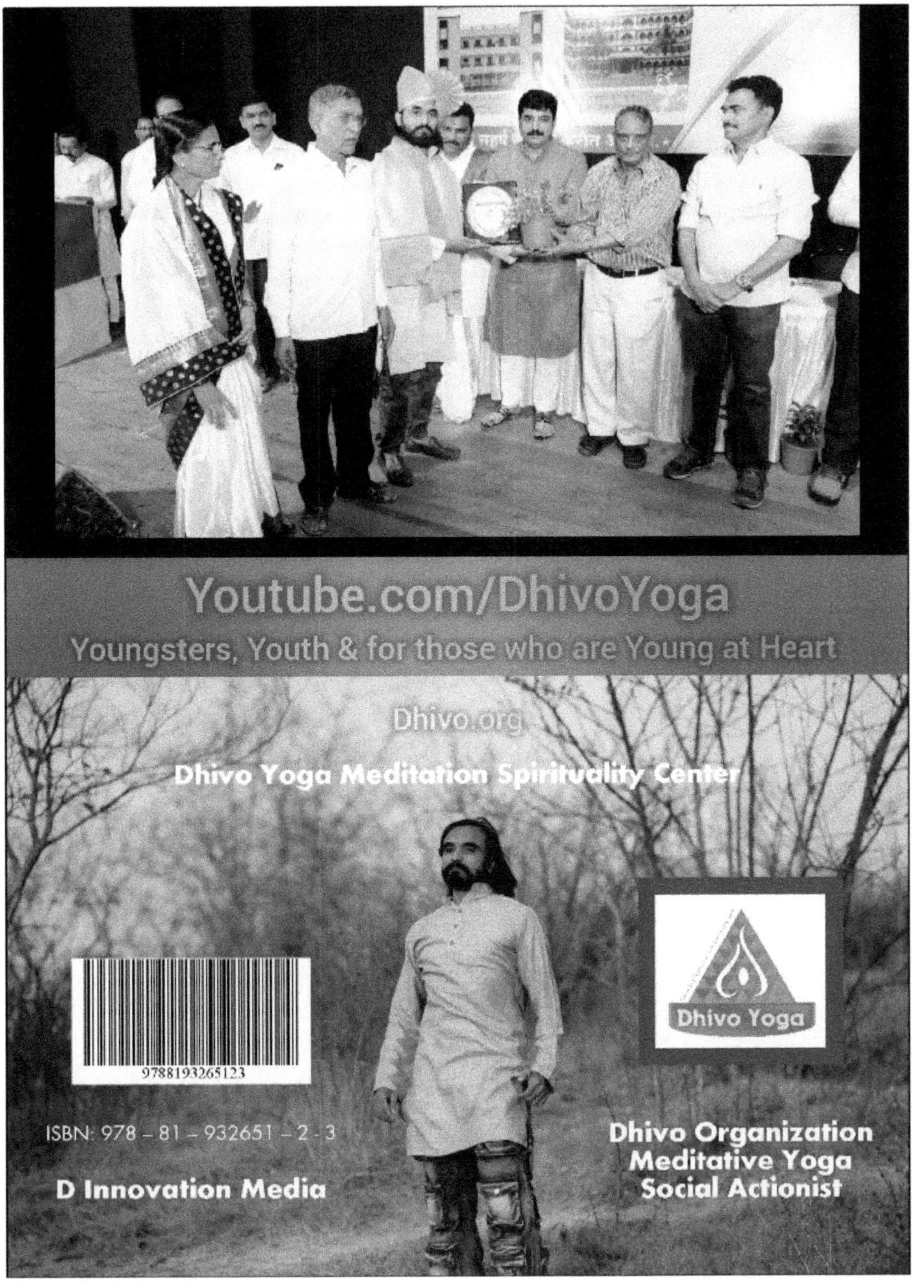
Youtube.com/DhivoYoga
Youngsters, Youth & for those who are Young at Heart
Dhivo.org
Dhivo Yoga Meditation Spirituality Center
Dhivo Yoga
9788193265123
ISBN: 978 - 81 - 932651 - 2 - 3
D Innovation Media
Dhivo Organization
Meditative Yoga
Social Actionist

www.ingramcontent.com/pod-product-compliance
Ingram Content Group UK Ltd.
Pitfield, Milton Keynes, MK11 3LW, UK
UKHW021407190726
13845UKWH00028B/928

9 788193 265123